# Cognitive Behavioral Therapy

*The Complete Psychologist's Guide to Rewiring Your Brain - Overcome Anxiety, Depression, and Phobias using Highly Effective Psychological Techniques*

# Table of Contents

# Introduction

It seems that even in today's modern world, where the quality of life is supposedly at its highest, there are people who are still not satisfied with their lives. There are those that seem to have everything they could ever wish for and they are still unhappy, depressed, stressed out, and have simply lost interest in life. These people struggle every day with feelings of self-doubt, worthlessness, and despair. It seems no matter what comes their way, they tend to fall into a quagmire of insecurities that keep them in a perpetual loop of fruitlessness which they are unable to disentangle themselves from no matter how hard they try.

These people usually go to their doctors for prescription medications just so they can get through the day ahead. The problem with this type of solution is that it's only temporary. As soon as the drug wears off, those negative feelings come flooding back. In essence, medication only masks the problem, but it doesn't get to the root cause of this epidemic which is affecting so many people.

Others may head off to a psychiatrist and express how they think or feel about their present state of mind. For years, this was the highly accepted form of treatment for those with chronic depressive or anxiety disorders, yet many of these sessions only address part of the problem. While this kind of treatment somewhat brings relief to patients, they often struggle with complex problems that may take years to overcome.

One relatively new form of alternative treatment that has been gaining popularity in recent years is Cognitive Behavioral Therapy, or CBT. This type of therapy sees the client as an individual who has developed a dysfunctional thought process that has a direct impact on his or her emotions and, by extension, their behavior. The result of this thought process eventually has a negative effect on their entire lives. It impacts their relationships, their professional life, their social position, and even their health.

The goal of CBT is to do more than just diagnose someone with a disorder as it also readjusts their thought processes into a more positive direction. It also determines how certain behaviors are creating insufficiencies in their lives and evaluates those negatives for frequency, intensity, and duration. If the behavior is determined to be excessive, techniques are deployed to decrease the frequency and/or intensity of that behavior. If it is determined to be an insufficiency, treatment will involve increasing the same elements.

Life can be a challenge for most people. It is perfectly normal to have bouts of anxiety, fearfulness, and depression from time to time. Most of us can shake off these negative feelings when they come upon us, but for some, they can linger for days, weeks, months, or years. It is in cases like these where the basic principles of CBT can be the most beneficial.

Quite often, those who seek out CBT already have had other forms of treatment but found that it was not enough to identify their problem, nor did countless hours of therapy sessions bring them relief. These treatments didn't give them what they needed to turn their life around and change the way they perceived the world around them.

Here, with the help of this book, we will attempt to guide you through the basic principles behind CBT and how it will equip you with techniques and strategies that can help you overcome the challenges that negative thinking can have on your life. You will learn:

- What CBT actually is and what are its underlying principles
- How and why it works
- What anxiety and depression really are and how CBT can help

- How to identify the underlying problem that triggers those negative feelings
- 4 different CBT methods worth trying
- How to determine if you can actually benefit from CBT

Whether you're reading this book for yourself or to gain additional information and help someone else, there is much to learn in these pages. Even if you determine that this type of therapy is not what you're looking for, there is a good chance that you'll learn a little more about yourself in the process. If you decide CBT is right for you, try the exercises included, create a plan that suits your needs, and jump right into the fray. Once you do, you'll be enlightened enough to look a little deeper. Perhaps you'll join the millions of others who have found a way to escape the vicious cycle of negative thinking and launch a whole new and more positive way of living that will benefit not just yourself, but everyone around you.

There are plenty of books on this subject on the market, thanks again for choosing this one! Every effort was made to ensure it is full of as much useful information as possible. Please enjoy!

# Chapter 1: What Is Cognitive Behavioral Therapy?

Just as in the field of medicine, modern science has helped us understand ourselves much better than we might have a few decades ago. With each new revelation into how our brain works, the field of psychology immediately adapts to the latest discovery. Cognitive behavioral therapy is the next evolutionary stage in psychotherapy.

Rather than laying on a sofa and pouring out your heart to a therapist discussing your feelings and emotions, with CBT, the patient would meet with a therapist and discuss specific problems he or she wanted to address. Common problems could range anywhere from having difficulty sleeping to extreme panic attacks.

With CBT, these problems then become the foundation for the following sessions when you and the therapist will have an open dialogue about how to best deal with them. In a typical session, you work with the therapist and decide on which of your goals to focus on during the coming week. The results of your efforts are usually the basis for discussion at the next session to determine the progress made and how well you completed your homework.

CBT sessions usually include a homework assignment that the patient can work on and complete before his next visit. This is a very important part of the entire process as it provides a connection between your actions during the week to the actual sessions you have with your therapist. You might be asked to keep a diary of events that trigger negative feelings and review them with each session. By doing this, you create a framework that may reveal an underlying cause for your negativity and give you the secret to how you can combat it.

There is a definite structure to CBT to make the most out of each therapy session. The structure ensures that every facet of the session reveals some intricacy in how the patient is responding to treatment. Each session may incorporate an open discussion, a review of the homework, and planning phase to lay the groundwork for the next time they meet. With each session, the patient will take on more and more responsibility for what's included, so, by the time they have their final meeting, the patient will feel as if he or she is empowered enough to continue the therapy on his own.

CBT also includes group sessions that allow a patient to share their struggles with those who may have the same or similar problems. These groups are usually mixed with some who are new to this type of program and others who have been in therapy for a long time. People who already have experience with CBT are a valuable source of advice as they can understand and can better relate to the same challenges their fellow patients may face.

## The goals of CBT

While there are similarities between CBT and other therapies, there are some striking differences that make it a preferred form of treatment over the other more traditional methods. Aside from the fact that the responsibility in each session is equally shared (gradually giving the patient the power to continue to progress even after the sessions are completed), the primary focus of CBT is to change one's thinking process. The focus is on adjusting the patient's beliefs and perceptions about the world around them and their role in it in a way that will facilitate both an emotional and behavioral change in their lives.

To accomplish this, there are specific goals that the therapist and patient must work together to accomplish:

- Encourage self-awareness and emotional intelligence by means of teaching them to read and understand their own emotions and to identify whether their feelings are healthy or not.

- Help them recognize how their own misconceptions and thoughts are the underlying force behind their negative and painful feelings.

- Reduce the negative symptoms they are experiencing by helping identify them. It puts them in the present by addressing the problems they are facing now.

- Giving them techniques that will help them identify and question their own negative thought patterns.

- Show them how to prevent future negative episodes that trigger emotional distress by helping them identify and change their core belief system which is responsible for their negative behavior.

With each successive session, the patient will be more and more empowered to manage their own negative feelings and alter their behavior, thus, gradually pulling them out of their own dysfunctional behavior and giving them a more productive life.

## Common problems that CBT addresses

When a person has chronic negative thinking, it can show up in a myriad of ways; many of them are not easily associated with depression or anxiety. Generally, CBT can help a host of different conditions because it works by teaching the patient to focus on very specific behaviors and goals. But CBT is not practical for those who have occasional bouts of negativity and frustration. This kind of behavior is normal for all people. It works best for anyone who has chronic problems in more extreme cases. CBT has been used to successfully resolve cases such as:

- Anger management
- Anxiety and depression
- Chronic fatigue syndrome
- Chronic pain
- Drug and/or alcohol abuse
- Eating disorders
- Unusual habits or quirks (such as facial tics and nervous twitching)
- Mood swings
- Obsessive-compulsive disorder
- Phobias
- PTSD (post-traumatic stress disorder)
- Relationship problems
- Insomnia

As news gets out about how successful CBT actually is, there is an increasing interest in the various forms of this type of psychotherapy. By learning the basic underlying principles of CBT, many have found that they can transition into a more open lifestyle that allows them to socialize and work better in a wide variety of settings.

## How it works

The success of CBT relies heavily on the strength of the relationship the patient has with their therapist. The best therapists do not expect the patient to depend on them to pull them out of their depressive state, but they work to empower them by teaching specific strategies they can use to pull themselves out.

In the early sessions, therapists will focus on understanding how the patient perceives the world around them, so they can create methods that can help them make changes. This is done by applying these basic principles:

- **There is a time limit**
  Unlike other forms of therapy where the sessions could last for months or even years, CBT sessions generally run for about 10 to 15 weekly sessions on average. This time limit has several benefits. First, it cuts back on the costs for the patient, but it also motivates them to work harder. There is no sense in putting it off for another week because at some point the sessions will come to an end.

- **It must be based on evidence**
  The techniques used in CBT are backed by extensive research and proven studies. Decisions on treatment are not based on guesswork or opinions, but instead, are based on the experiences of thousands of others who have gone through it before. Even the estimation of how long a treatment should last needs to be based on empirical evidence.

- **Each session is focused on the patient's goals**
  Goals are not given arbitrarily, but the patient sets their own goals that they want to address in the here and now. The patient is also given the chance to gauge whether the therapy is helping them meet their goals or not.

- **The entire process is collaborative**
  This means that responsibility for fixing the behavior does not lie entirely on the therapist, but it is a combined effort designed to meet the patient's unique set of needs.

To better understand this, cognitive behavioral therapy is not just one single type of therapy, but it encompasses various types of therapy in a single package. By incorporating more than one technique into CBT, it can be adapted to deal with a wide variety of anxiety and stress-related issues including obsessive-compulsive disorder (OCD), post-traumatic stress disorder (PTSD), and even personality disorders.

## Why is it effective?

There is much debate on the reason why CBT is so effective, but a general consensus lies in the basic principles behind it. As we come to have a better understanding of the relationship we all have between our thoughts and feelings and our actions, we begin to realize that treatment of the whole body must include addressing our mental consciousness. Not that this is new information to most of us, but by disrupting the negative thought patterns and replacing them with positive ones, we can change behavior without actually having to address the behavior at all.

When someone feels the pressure of anxiety on them, they usually feel as if they have no control over what is happening in their lives. The therapy introduced through CBT helps them narrow down a specific point of attack. Rather than attempting to address every issue, a CBT session will focus on a single issue with targeted exercises designed to focus completely on improving that one single area in their life.

The 'homework' element helps them practice the new skills they have learned and enhances their understanding of how their thoughts are actually driving their behavior. By producing a better pattern of thinking, this breaks up the vicious cycle they're in where their thoughts and feelings are working against them, which literally reinforces their new actions so that they're focused in a different direction.

## A brief history of CBT

Cognitive behavioral therapy has been around for several decades. The therapy was first introduced in the 1960s by Dr. Aaron T. Beck of the University of Pennsylvania. After studying and practicing psychoanalysis for many years, he wanted to support his conclusions on the concept of depression with the experiments he designed.

To his surprise, however, the research he accumulated did not support his fundamental concepts about depression and, in fact, proved the opposite. This made him look for different ways to conceptualize depression. He learned that depressed patients spoke of streams of negative thoughts that seemed to just pop up without warning. He referred to these as 'automatic thoughts' and labeled them in three separate categories:

- Negative thoughts about themselves
- Negative thoughts about the world

- Negative thoughts about the future

He continued his research by helping patients identify these automatic thoughts and evaluate them. In this process, patients became more aware of their thought patterns and were better able to change their views and think in more realistic terms about their lives. As a result, they became more emotionally stable, and their behavior started to improve.

When his patients started to change their personal beliefs, a natural consequence was that a long-lasting behavior change followed. Dr. Beck referred to this as 'cognitive therapy.'

Since then, more than a thousand different studies on CBT have been completed to prove just how effective it has been in treating psychiatric disorders, psychological problems, and even medical conditions found to be associated with various psychological components.

# Chapter 2: A Closer Look at Anxiety and Depression

To get a better understanding of how CBT works, we must get a clearer understanding of how our mind works in general. When we have thoughts, they usually fly through our minds in a tiny fraction of a second; quite often we don't even realize that we've had a thought, let alone the effects it has on our behavior.

So, when you lose a loved one in death, lose your job, deal with a family break-up, or have some other traumatic situation, you are quite likely to feel some level of sadness or even fear about what's in store for your future. These are pretty normal reactions to devastating events in our lives. We don't realize that these feelings and the behaviors that follow are a direct result of our thoughts. Most people will bounce back in time and get back to living life. However, for some, these low emotional states tend to be more intense and can linger for extended periods of time.

## What is depression?

Depression, which tends to occur more in women than in men, is the direct result of these lingering thoughts. The way it manifests itself can vary depending on a person's age and gender. In men, it may be seen in symptoms such as tiredness, irritability, and sometimes anger. Men tend to behave more recklessly when they are depressed, which can be seen by their abuse of drugs or alcohol. These behaviors may often be passed off as masculine, so they are less likely to recognize it as depression and are not inclined to seek help or treatment.

Women in a depressed state are more likely to appear sad and have deep feelings of worthlessness and guilt. They may be reluctant to take part in social activities or engage with others, even those who are close to them. Depression in children will also be different. Young children may refuse to go to school or show signs of separation anxiety when parents leave.  Teenagers are more likely to be irritable, sulky, and often get into trouble in school. In more extreme cases, you might see signs of an eating disorder or substance abuse.

## Types of depression

Depression often comes in degrees with several different types that we should be aware of. These different types may have many similarities, but you will also find they each have their own unique symptoms that set them apart.

### Major depressive disorder

This condition can be identified when at least five of the following symptoms are present:

- An overwhelming feeling of sadness
- A loss of interest in normal, everyday activities
- Decrease in appetite
- Insomnia/hypersomnia
- Psychomotor agitation
- Chronic fatigue
- Feelings of worthlessness
- Excessive guilt
- Recurrent thoughts of death or suicide
- Diminished ability to think

Any of these symptoms that last for more than two weeks or create a major divergence from normal behavior could be considered as the development of a major depressive disorder.

**Persistent depressive disorder (dysthymia)**
This is characterized by an overwhelmingly sad mood that is persistently present for the majority of a two-year period (one year for children and adolescents). They should also have at least two of the following symptoms:

- Poor appetite
- Overeating
- Insomnia/hypersomnia
- Fatigue
- Low self-esteem

- Poor concentration
- Feelings of hopelessness
- Has trouble making decisions

The symptoms of a persistent depressive disorder may be the same as that of a major depressive disorder but are generally milder.

There are various kinds of depressive disorders that could be remedied by CBT. The symptoms are often very similar in their degrees of intensity. If you recognize some of these symptoms in yourself or in someone you know, it is strongly recommended that you seek a professional diagnosis and start treatment as soon as possible, so you can get back to living a normal and productive life.

## What is anxiety?

Closely associated with depression is anxiety, which can manifest itself in a variety of ways. A mild case of anxiety might be evidenced by the sensation of butterflies in the stomach in anticipation of an important event, concern about meeting deadlines, or nervousness about an anticipated treatment or procedure.

For most people, when anxiety is present, they can just ride it out. It is a normal part of life. However, there are some types of anxiety that are far from the norm. Some anxieties can trigger fears (spiders, snakes, planes, etc.) or phobias that are excessive and irrational fears. Many people have a fear of snakes even though they have never actually come in contact with one. Others are afraid of dogs even though they have never had a bad experience with one. This type of anxiety easily develops into an anxiety disorder.

To help in differentiating between normal anxiety and an anxiety disorder, first take a close look at the cause of the anxiety. Then look at the instinctive response to that fear. If the behavior is considered realistic, then it is probably 'normal' anxiety. However, if the response is viewed as extreme enough to disrupt normal life, it could be classified as an anxiety disorder.

For example, you may be anxious about getting sick, so you take steps to prevent illness. You may use hand sanitizer, regularly wash your hands, or even avoid shaking hands with people in public places. This is a normal form of anxiety. On the other hand, if your fear of getting sick is so strong that you don't want to leave your home or you are constantly washing and cleaning, you may have an anxiety disorder.

There are many different types of anxiety-related disorders out there, and for your convenience, these disorders have been grouped into three different categories:

- **Anxiety disorders**

  An excessive fear of a real or perceived threat

- **Obsessive-compulsive disorders**

  Intrusive fearful thoughts that trigger compulsive behaviors

- **Trauma/stressor-related disorders**

  The extreme reaction to a past traumatic or stress-related event

If you suspect you or someone you know has an anxiety disorder and is struggling to overcome the symptoms, CBT is one way to help. This method of helping patients identify the thought process that triggers the fear may be the best solution to the problem.

## How CBT can help

By mastering the techniques in CBT, those with anxiety or depressive disorders can learn how to control those fears and the behaviors they trigger. The program will help to establish clear-cut goals to work on, teach them how to identify the thoughts that start the process, and arm them with defense mechanisms to fight these behaviors.

CBT helps by providing completely new ways to process those thoughts, feelings, and behaviors, so the patients can better cope with these normal events that happen in life. Instead of reacting negatively to traumatic events, it gives them the ability to reframe the triggering event and experience it from an entirely new perspective.

# Chapter 3: Identifying the Underlying Problem

In CBT, one of the first things you must do is to identify the underlying problem which triggers the negative and unwanted behavior. This is a crucial part of the therapy as it gives you an area to focus all your effort on. It also gives you purpose while you learn how to manage your feelings of anxiety and depression.

It is important to understand that people are not exactly alike, even if they have been diagnosed with the same disorder. This makes it very important that every CBT session is tailored to meet the unique needs of the individual. There is no blanket rule that will apply in every situation. For that reason, in order to identify the underlying cause for the negative behavior, you must first get a clear picture of how those negative thoughts fit into the entire picture of life.

In the initial visit with the therapist, you will probably be asked a series of questions. One of the first things you and the therapist will work on together is establishing goals. The therapist may not come right out and ask, "What are your goals?" or, "What do you want?" but instead may ask something less obvious, a question that will compel you to think deeply about your answer. For example, they may ask you what your reason is for seeking therapy, or why you feel you need help.

The reason for this is that we are rarely honest with ourselves. The first answer that comes to mind doesn't even address or identify the true nature of our problems. The real answers are often buried deep inside of us, and without some serious inward analysis of ourselves, the true answers may never actually come to the fore.

You could answer this question with the obvious. Many might respond with, "My wife told me to come," or, "I need help," but those answers don't really explain the real reason why you came. Chances are, if your wife told you to come, it is most likely because you are demonstrating certain behaviors she finds disturbing. This is a good reason for you to sit down and seriously consider why you're seeking out a therapist as that could be the first step in helping you get down to the root of your problem.

## How to identify negative thought patterns when they present themselves

Chances are, even after the initial session, you may not have gotten to the core of your problem, but you will begin to think a little differently about identifying it. Whatever your problem is, you've gotten pretty good at covering it up, or you overcame it at some point. You also need to identify those tactics you used to handle your behavior, and the odds are high that if you look underneath these strong points you put forward every day, you'll find the root of your problem.

In this period of retrospection, it's important to take an honest view of your life and where you're heading. Look closely at how your anxiety and depression are affecting your behavior. Again, you have to start looking below the surface to reveal these behaviors, which may be obvious to other people, but it may not be so apparent to you. Your negative behavior may appear in different areas of your life.

- **Relationships**
  Some may be struggling with a difficult marriage. However, the underlying problem is not necessarily the marriage but in behaviors demonstrated in the marriage. If you're depressed, that may present itself as being very irritable, distant, or uninterested. Whether you're talking about a marriage, parent/child relationship, or a friendship, these kinds of behaviors over an extended period of time can really cause damage to a strong bond.

Anxiety also is not easily identified in your relationship. Without knowing how it is affecting you, it can be very difficult to see. Neither anxiety nor depression have clear signs that say, "I'm anxious or stressed," or, "This is me being depressed." They are hidden emotions that appear in a myriad of ways that affect your behavior.

You may have lost someone many years ago, friends moved away, lost some jobs, or trust was broken. These things do not have to be recent, as they can be experiences buried deep in your subconscious. However, since they were never addressed, these experiences are resurfacing to damage your present life.

- **Career**
How you behave at work can reveal many things about yourself. Whether you're a work-at-home mom, or you're a corporate executive, if you have unidentified anxiety and depression, your relationships at work are going to suffer. Are you happy with your work? Do you wake up eager to get started, or do you feel like it is nothing but a tiresome chore, and you feel too unmotivated to perform your tasks?

Some people feel as if they are overworked, others may feel bored, and others may feel unfulfilled. Often, issues with money come up when thinking about work. You may thoroughly enjoy your work but are not satisfied because the money is not enough, or you may be working on a job that you hate because it pays the money you need. Understanding these things will help you identify the underlying problem hidden beneath the surface.

- **Spirituality**

There is a big difference between having spirituality and having a religion. Many people feel this is the same and struggle with the inner self as a result. Religion is the belief of certain tenets, or teachings, whereas spirituality is what gives your life purpose.

How are you meeting that spiritual need? Most people find it by connecting to something more powerful than themselves, such as a 'supreme being of the universe.' Other people fulfill it through humanitarian efforts. If your spiritual self is not being fulfilled, it can leave you with a feeling of emptiness that no amount of money, relationship, or status in life can fill. Our personal sense of identity is closely connected to this, so it is well worth contemplating where we are in respect to our spirituality.

- **Physical well-being**

  Our physical health can also have an impact on our behavior. When we are not strong and healthy, it can have a deep impact on our emotions and mental state of mind. Even if we are relatively strong but are not physically active, it can have a strong negative impact on us. If you are dealing with chronic health problems, or you're just too busy to maintain your physical health, it could be the trigger to many of your negative behaviors.

- **Drugs and alcohol**

  Any kind of mood-altering substances can greatly affect your thought processes. If you find that you need to infuse yourself regularly with drugs, alcohol, or any other substance to get through the day, it could be a sign of depression or anxiety. Try to think if any of your family or friends pointed out that you might have a problem. Do you come home every day needing a drink? While you may not be an 'alcoholic,' as some may think, your depression or anxiety may have led you to develop a dependence on these substances in order to cope with the daily stress of life.

- **Food**

  Many people are stress eaters. They eat because they are stressed, unhappy, or bored. How does eating make you feel? Other people may have other fears that may be evident in their relationship with food. A poor self-image could cause you to not eat for fear of gaining too much weight. A poor self-image could also cause you to overeat, as you see it as comfort food, the only thing you have that makes you feel good.

- **Rest**

  The body is a highly efficient machine, but it can't run indefinitely. Like all machines, it needs to be refueled, and it needs to rest. If you're not getting enough rest every day or sleeping too much, this can cause problems. Some people naturally wake up the moment the sun rises, while others have to put up a struggle just to wake up. Others may fall asleep quickly but wake up in the middle of the night and cannot fall back to sleep again.

  What keeps you from getting your rest? Noisy dogs in the neighborhood, loud music, traffic, children, snoring, health problems, or worry? Many of these things could be perfectly normal, while others could be a sign of anxiety or depression.

- **Recreation**

   Everyone needs downtime from the rigors of daily life. If we have become so busy that we have no time to unwind or enjoy life, our mental state can suffer. Our brains and our bodies need to recharge to stay balanced. Many people who work second jobs to take care of their financial responsibilities or are constantly moving from sunrise to sunset so they can manage the necessary things in life, will eventually suffer from anxiety or depression.

   If you have no free time or can't find time to slow down and relax, eventually, it will take its toll on you. Even if you have free time, but you can't let your mind relax, you are always thinking of the next task you've got to do, and you can't enjoy your break, this could be a trigger that is causing your negative behavior.

Hopefully, these points have made you look deeper into yourself and your behavior to help you identify the underlying triggers behind your negative behavior. After this type of contemplation, your mind is probably spinning in different directions. Now is the time to set some goals that will help you get your life back on track.

## Setting goals

As you went through the list, you probably saw signs of anxiety and depression in your behavior that you had never noticed before. So, you now have a clearer picture of the things you'd like to change.

It is difficult to set goals when you don't know yourself or what your real problem is, but once you've gone through these points, you'll have a clear and honest picture of who you really are and, hopefully, a good idea of how you'd like to change. So, what is it about you that needs to be adjusted so that your behavioral patterns can become more positive?

When it comes to developing your goals, use these points to help you. Don't just think about what you'd like to do. Our behavior can only change when our thinking changes. So, think in terms of how you want to adjust your life and how you feel about different things.

While the words of those close to you may weigh on your mind, you must think in terms of what you want to achieve. This is your life, and the goals must be yours. If you are reflecting someone else's wants and desires, you'll quickly lose interest, and before long, you'll give up.

The goals you set will be the basis for each session you have, and it will also serve as the foundation for a plan that will help you change your thought processes and behavior. Throughout the rest of this program, you will refer to your goal list several times a week, make adjustments, and as long as you follow through, you will see modest changes take effect very quickly.

## How to replace poor coping strategies with more effective ones

There are many things that can cause depression and anxiety. Circumstances that are beyond our control can take away our feeling of autonomy, that feeling that we are not in control and that we don't have the freedom to make our own choices. There are three things that we must have in our lives to give us satisfaction: autonomy, connections, and abilities. When these things are prominent in our lives, we are happier and have a greater sense of fulfillment. When they are absent, negative feelings begin to appear. We feel ashamed though we've done nothing wrong, we feel depressed, and if we don't have those connections our psychological mind craves, loneliness sets in.

Many who seek out CBT often complain about similar feelings. They are usually in high-stress situations, they do not feel recognized or appreciated for the things they do, and are often isolated from those people they truly want in their lives. When that happens, their energy levels begin to drop, and the mental, emotional, and spiritual side of them starts to starve. This is the point when changing behavior is crucial to healing the whole person. It's time to focus on the positive behavior needed in order to set things right.

You might be wondering if these negative behaviors are triggered by our thoughts. Why exactly do we even need to focus on behavior in therapy? This is a logical question and certainly deserves discussion. First, getting people to do things they enjoy is far simpler than getting them to change their viewpoints. For example, getting people to stay within the speed limit is a lot easier than getting them to believe that there is a legitimate reason for the law. Many will comply with the law to avoid getting a ticket, but that doesn't necessarily mean they believe it is justified.

Another important fact to consider is that it instantly addresses those innate needs we all have. By making small adjustments in behavior, such as getting people to do things they thoroughly enjoy, we can get the brain to produce endorphins and trigger an antidepressant effect.

Besides all of that, it can work on our inner thoughts and help dispel some of the negative thinking that our minds are stuck in. This aspect of therapy is referred to as 'behavioral activation' and focuses on changing your actions to do something more positive.

At this point, you've simply identified that you feel anxious and depressed. You may not know exactly what makes you feel this way, but it is really unimportant. The key component here is that you have to start doing things that give you enjoyment and pull yourself out of the rut you're in.

The reason for this is because there could be a thousand things buried deep in your psyche that could trigger depression, but it's your response to this negative feeling that is causing the behavior. It is normal for a depressed person to isolate themselves, almost as if they were punishing themselves for feeling emotions. They don't speak to their friends or family, they stop doing the things they enjoy, and they fail to find purpose in anything that they do.

We've already determined that both depression and anxiety are standard aspects of life, so what makes us depressed today may not be the same thing tomorrow. We need to teach ourselves the proper way to respond to these negative events when they occur. When we do things that infuse us with positive energy, things slowly begin to change.

When it comes to choosing positive activities that will instill good feelings, they can't be activities that someone else believes is important for you. This is why answering the questions above is beneficial in helping you decide on which activities will work best. They must be based on your personal goals and what you see as vital to building yourself up. If the activities are prescribed based on your therapist's views or those of someone close to you, it is possible they will work for a little while, but you'll eventually fall back into your depressive state again.

For that reason, you are the only person who is capable of creating this plan of action. Take your time with this as it must be based on the things that you think are the most important to you and will give you that sense of purpose, value, and worthiness.

## Short-term vs. long-term rewards

Even though doing things we enjoy is easier, for someone who is dealing with anxiety and depression, it can be quite a challenge. It is pretty simple to write down on a piece of paper that you want to spend more time with family and friends, but it is another thing to break the negative cycle you're in.

To accomplish this, you need to look at both the short-term and the long-term rewards. Most will reach out for the short-term rewards because they get immediate satisfaction. For example, you receive an invitation to go to the movies with friends. Your immediate reaction is to take advantage of the short-term rewards and hibernate in your home instead. You can watch your favorite TV show on Netflix and just chill out. You might be thinking, "It's too much of a bother to get dressed and go out. I could stay home and just watch some TV. I have food in my fridge."

In this scenario, you feel very comfortable in your little cocoon, and you don't want to deal with the stress involved with leaving it. It is your safe place, and you are content with putting yourself there. However, if your goals are set to open up and let more people into your life, you'll change your behavior and join your friends for dinner and a movie. After all, you do enjoy movies and spending time with your friends.

If you choose short-term rewards, you'll feel good for an evening, perhaps even a day, but it wouldn't get you any closer to your goals. Later, you'll feel even worse because you knew you really wanted to go out with your friends anyway. So, how do we learn how to choose long-term goals over the short-term ones? There are some basic strategies we can try:

- Go back to your list of goals you created and choose which ones you value the most.

- Create a list of activities that support those values.

- Make a plan to incorporate those activities into your routine. It could look something like this: "I value living in a beautiful home."

- Clean my living room so I'll feel comfortable having people over.

- Get my decorating kit and add some color to my house.

You may reach a point where you actually complete the positive activities you have on your list, but there should never be a point where you actually meet your values 100%. Values will always have something that you need to work on, whereas activities are the actions that you do to satisfy your values. It's a good idea to create a list of those things that you consider to be important in your life. Again, for everyone it is different, so when you create this list, think only of the things that you think are important and make you feel good.

You can create a value and activity list for each of those categories we discussed earlier, so you have a positive action plan for every aspect of your life. It doesn't really matter what your values are; at this point, your focus should be on creating a list of activities that will help you fortify these values in your mind. It's quite possible that you won't be able to complete your list of values in a single sitting, and as you go through your days, you will likely think of more to add to your list.

When it comes down to the activities you want to do, you can list them in order of importance. The activities that are more important should be placed at the top of your list, while those that are the least important, even though they give you a certain level of enjoyment, can be put further down on your list. For example, chores are usually important, but clubbing is not. Make sure your list has a nice balance, so that not only can you can get the important things done, but you will still have enough pleasurable activities to do as well.

Once your list is done, it's time to start making these activities a priority in your life. If you've already listed them in order of importance, then you know what activities you need to do first. However, you can take another approach to accomplish this. You could order it based on the level of difficulty, from the easiest to hardest.

This will help with getting things done quickly to boost your confidence level and make you more emboldened to tackle those activities that you think are more difficult.

Regardless of which approach you take, you won't be able to tackle it all at the same time. CBT is a progressive approach to negative behavior. By starting with those tasks that won't require special effort to accomplish, you reinforce your mental and spiritual self so that, in time, the more difficult activities will feel like they are within reach.

## Consider obstacles

Before you start jumping in and trying to do things, realize that you're going to face obstacles along the way. Our mind is infamous for playing tricks on us, especially when we're stuck in a negative thought process. If your goal is to have family and friends over, your mind will inevitably start throwing up negative curveballs. "They don't want to spend time with me, they're too busy. They have more important things they care about. They live too far away." All of these negative thoughts present a stumbling block that could be thrown in your path. It helps to prepare for these negativities before you even start.

Once you start, you'll begin building up a momentum towards more positive behavior, and any one of these negative thoughts is like an oil slick on a race track. Develop a plan to get around them before you begin. You don't want to ignore these obstacles when they come up, but you want to have a plan to address them when they appear. Otherwise, your life could start spinning completely out of control.

For example, "They don't want to spend time with me." This is a negative thought that you can address beforehand. You can overcome this obstacle by finding ways to prove to yourself that this is not true. Perhaps an activity you can devise is to call someone in your family and extend an invitation. Once you hear how happy they are to hear from you, your negative feelings will start to fade. By performing another activity that will counteract those negative thoughts, you can successfully find a way to navigate around those obstacles in order to reach your goals.

Another strategy you can apply is to give yourself a reward when you accomplish each activity. This is very important when you're trying to complete activities which are more important than enjoyable. Cleaning your house for having friends over is not usually a pleasurable activity to keep you motivated, but a reward will give you a certain level of satisfaction to makc it worthwhile.

## Make a schedule

It is also important that you give yourself a time limit to accomplish these activities. Since the activities go against your natural instinct to be negative, if you don't have a specific time frame in which to complete them, you are very likely to fall into the habit of procrastination. The idea that you can put it off until later can be an easy trap to fall into.

## Create accountability

If you've been in a depressive state for a long time, you're probably not accustomed to having another person held accountable for the things you do. But these activities will pose a challenge for you, and if you allow your negative thinking to get in the way, it will be easy to just dismiss them unless you have someone or something that you have to answer to.

Accountability could be anything from telling someone what your goals and activities are, to keeping a journal detailing what you expect to do, when, and how you're going to do it. If you're responsible enough to make yourself accountable, then keeping a daily diary or a journal may be enough to keep you pushing in the right direction, but if it's not, find a buddy. This could be your spouse, your parents, or your co-worker, so you have someone to answer to if you don't complete your tasks.

# Identifying patterns of thought

A big part of CBT is the analysis phase of everything you do. No matter which type of CBT therapy you choose to use, you will always conclude these by analyzing the results you've learned. If you're looking back after trying to implement the activities you set out for yourself, your next therapy session will be geared towards reviewing those activities and determining what actions went right and what actions went wrong.

Even if things didn't go as you would have hoped, there are positive lessons you can glean from the experience. It is up to you and the therapist to find and reinforce those positive elements of your efforts. Your change in behavior may not yield big changes right away, but the good things in life often come in small packages. In time, these will amount to a big difference in your life.

Still, even in these circumstances where things are going smoothly, many of the emotional reactions that we experience are a direct result of how we perceive a particular situation and not the situation itself. If we are in the habit of thinking negatively, we probably have already developed the habit of thinking irrationally about these issues.

This is the body's natural attempt to make sense of the world we live in. If you lose your job, your mind will automatically make up a story to explain what happened. If that story becomes our belief, we will have an emotional reaction to it, no matter what the truth really is. As a result, we need to stop, analyze the situation, and question whether our assumptions are reasonable or not. We need to practice how to identify our thought patterns, analyze them, and course correct whenever needed, especially if we've drifted off into irrational territory.

It may take time to develop this skill, but as you evaluate your own experiences, you should take note of certain things that can help you determine if you're having a single negative thought or if you've developed a pattern of thinking that is affecting your behavior.

## Is there a specific time or event that triggers your depressive or anxious behavior?

Sometimes it may be difficult to recall a specific thought as the main cause of your behavior. When that happens, it is usually because you don't have enough information for the thoughts to become evident. When you're in a depressed or anxious state of mind, it is easy to forget elements of a particular situation. You may not be able to identify the specific thought that triggered an emotion you had a week ago.

This is not a skill that everyone possesses, but it will be very important to develop that skill and practice it over time. You can do this by keeping a record of instances when your mood changed. Just get into the habit of writing down what happened, what you thought, and how you felt about it. If you make a habit of doing this, in time, you'll be able to recall your thoughts for almost every event you experience.

When that happens, you'll be able to identify certain patterns in your thinking and visually identify exactly which negative thoughts are causing the problem. You might recognize some of the more common thoughts that trigger abnormal behavior which cause anxiety and depression.

Common fears as a result of anxiety:

- **Phobias**
  An irrational fear of something

- **Panic**
  An irrational fear of a dangerous event

- **Social anxiety**
  Fear of doing something embarrassing

- **Generalized anxiety disorder**
  The "what if..." fear

Common triggers as a result of depression:
- Feelings of worthlessness
- Feeling vulnerable
- Feeling incompetent
- Hopelessness

Of course, these are not the only patterns of thought you can discover, but they are some of the most common ones. Being able to identify these threads that are running through your mind can be very effective in giving you a plan of action to counteract these negative thoughts.

As you go through the initial phases of cognitive behavioral therapy, your primary goal is to identify the root cause of your problem, so you can address the issues and course correct. There are numerous ways to break up these negative tendencies in your life, and, depending on how severe your problem is or what damage it has caused, other methods may work better for you. In the next chapters, we'll look a bit more closely at some of these methods and how they work.

# Chapter 4: The Multimodal Model (MMT)

There are many ways to help someone adjust their negative behavioral patterns with CBT. In multimodal coaching, the emphasis is placed on the distinct dimensions of the human personality:

- **Behavior**
  These are the traits that an individual may present

- **Effect**
  Positive or negative influence on our emotions

- **Sensation**
  Automatic sensations in our bodies such as sweating, heart racing, tension, etc.

- **Imagery**
  Mental pictures

- **Cognition**
  Our thought processes

- **Interpersonal – relationship**

- **Biological intervention**

These aspects can be easily remembered by using the acronym BASIC ID. While all people experience these same dimensions in one form or another, it also has room to address the uniqueness of each individual. You can think of it in the same way music is composed. Music is always composed of the same notes on the scale, yet, no two musical pieces are exactly alike. The same is true for the billions of people who have these seven dimensions in their personality; you may find some that are similar, but none of them is exactly the same as another.

The goal of the MMD is to help the individual make the changes necessary to move them from their current personality to become a more progressive and better individual. It is not likely that any of us will reach our full potential. However, by applying the MMD model, it can help us pinpoint the areas in our personality that may need adjusting and help us make those changes.

In this type of therapy, the patient is asked a series of questions relating to these modalities to help determine exactly what kind of help they need. For example:

**Behavior:** What behavior would you like to see more or less of?

**Effect:** What emotion do you want to change?

**Sensation:** What sensations would you like to eliminate or would you like to experience more?

**Imagery:** What would you prefer to see in your mind's eye?

**Cognition:** What thoughts would you like to have? Which ones would you like to start or stop?

**Interpersonal relationships:** What kind of changes would you like to make socially?

**Biological intervention:** What health habits or physical issues would you like to overcome?

The answers to these questions will help the therapist and patient determine a set of goals, a course of action, and a timeline. It doesn't matter what the answers to the questions are, as they are specifically designed to help the patient see exactly where they are in terms of their psychological, emotional, and spiritual condition. Obviously, the more detailed the answers are, the easier it will be for both of them to identify a course of action that's beneficial. With each passing goal achieved, the patient moves closer to becoming the kind of person they want to be.

The more you are aware of your BASIC ID, the easier it will be to recognize negative behavior patterns when they arise, and the easier it will be to implement strategies that will help them change.

## Who can benefit from MMT?

MMT is primarily used when there are very complex cases dealing with depression or performance anxiety. These are people whose negative behavior has put their careers or family life in jeopardy. Because their fear or anxiety has reached such a point that it affects all dimensions of their personality, an intervention on an extensive level may be necessary.

The general principle behind MMT is to optimize therapy by approaching multiple issues simultaneously. A person who is dependent on drugs may also be struggling with interpersonal relationships. They may be coping with health problems as they try to handle their emotional issues. With MMT, it is quite possible for them to receive an effective and productive remedy to all their psychological issues, thus speeding up their recovery time.

# Chapter 5: Eye Movement Desensitization and Reprocessing Therapy (EMDR)

'Eye Movement Desensitization and Reprocessing' therapy (EMDR) is a form of therapy specifically developed to help people who are suffering from traumatic events. Traumatic memories or images may pop up in their minds without warning, triggering all sorts of negative emotions and actions. EMDR makes it easy to access the part of the brain that processes these images or memories and helps them to resolve the issues that are triggering them.

Through EMDR, people learn that the mind can actually heal itself from psychological trauma in much the same way as the body can heal from physical trauma. By learning how the body heals from physical trauma, such as a cut or a break, you can begin to understand how the mind automatically works to repair itself. If the location of a previous injury is repeatedly injured, the pain will recur. However, once the object that caused the injury is removed, and the threat has passed, the body will immediately begin to heal.

With EMDR therapy, we see that psychological trauma can be healed in the same way. The brain actually wants to be mentally healthy, but if the system continues to be blocked by repeated recurrences of the traumatic event, it can leave a lasting scar which can cause a great deal of suffering. However, once the imbalance is removed, the mind can begin to heal itself.

During therapy sessions, the patient generally must address emotionally disturbing material and some form of external stimulus at the same time.
Once therapy has been completed, the patient can find relief from their own negative beliefs and can move on to more positive things in their life. This healing is all done through a detailed series of protocols and procedures designed to activate the brain's natural healing process.

## How does it work?

There are eight phases of EMDR treatment. Eye movement and other types of exercises that promote bilateral stimulation encompass a significant part of the session. The clinician will first pinpoint the memory that is triggering the negative behavior by asking the patient to recall various aspects of the traumatic event in mind. At the same time, the clinician will have the patient track his hand movements as it crosses the patient's field of vision.

This will cause the client's mind to process the memory and the feelings that are associated with it, thus triggering a shift in their emotions. For example, a rape victim may associate a feeling of disgust or horror in recalling the event, but after the shift takes place, could demonstrate positive feelings of survival and strength.

All of this is done without the need for a lot of talking. Therefore, the results of this type of therapy do not stem from a conclusion that the clinician has gleaned from the talk but instead from the patient's own internal intellectual and emotional processes. The result is that a patient will leave the session feeling empowered by the same traumatic event that originally had broken them.

In this type of therapy, the damage created by the traumatic event didn't just heal the patient, it literally transformed them. The patient's thoughts, their feelings, and their behavior are part of a delicate balance of emotional and mental health.

## What to expect

EMDR therapy concentrates on three different time periods: past, present, and future. Initially, the focus will be concentrated on the past when the traumatic event occurred. After that, the focus will shift to the present, identifying situations which cause additional distress. Patients will be given the tools to develop their own set of skills and attitudes they can use to change their behaviors so that they can get a more positive result.

**Phase 1**

This concentrates on the history. The therapist and client will work together to identify potential target events in the past where they can apply EMDR therapy. This could include memories of traumatic or distressing events and situations that cause continued distress. But the focus is not so much on the event as it is on finding the right tools to combat the negative responses the events triggered. The session may start with an examination of childhood events and then progress to more current stressors until the offending event is identified.

**Phase 2**

The patient is given different tools to help them manage their emotional distress. These could be in the form of imagery exercises or stress reduction techniques that can be used when memories of these events come up. The goal here is to arm them with something that will provide an effective way to change and restore the balance of their mental health.

**Phase 3-6**

The EMDR therapy is applied. First, the visual imagery of the event is recalled. This triggers the negative belief, which will trigger the negative emotions and body sensations.

The patient will follow that negative belief with a positive one, and the therapist will help him or her describe the intensity of the negative emotions. After this, the EDMR process will begin where the patient is asked to focus on the negative imagery, the thoughts associated with it, and the sensations that are happening in the body while the therapist proceeds with the EMDR process.

The EMDR process could include eye movements, a series of tapping rhythms, or playing a sequence of tones. It will be different for everyone as not everything can be measured in the same way. While this is going on, the patient is then asked to just be an observer of what spontaneously happens.

At the conclusion of each session, the patient is asked to allow their minds to go blank and observe the thoughts, emotions, memories, and images that spring from the memory. With each of these sets of directed focus, the patient will come to understand more about their thought process. If, at any point, they become too distressed or are no longer able to make progress, the therapist will give the patient additional assistance to help them get back on track.

If the client doesn't demonstrate distress from the targeted memory, they will then be asked to recall the positive belief they had when the session started. The session will then shift towards the positive belief and making whatever adjustments are necessary. The first traumatic event has been addressed successfully, so they will then focus their efforts on the next traumatic event in the patient's history.

**Phase 7**

The therapist will ask the patient to keep a running log or a journal for the following week to record any related events or information that may come up in-between sessions. When these come up, the patient will need to recall the self-calming activities that they learned back in phase 2.

**Phase 8**

This is where a review and an examination are made on the progress throughout each of the sessions. Then, the patient will be instructed on how to handle any future events that may trigger negative behavior and how to respond to them when they come up.

When implemented correctly, many people who suffer from major traumatic events in their past will learn how to redirect their minds and guide them in the best way to handle those negative thoughts and feelings that often come unbidden to the surface. This type of psychotherapy makes it possible for people to heal from all sorts of extreme emotional distress and disturbing life experiences and move on from there to a more positive and rewarding future.

# Chapter 6: Rational Emotive Behavior Therapy Method (REBT)

'Rational Emotive Behavior Therapy,' or REBT, is very different from other forms of psychotherapy in that it places a great deal of importance on how a patient is thinking. It reinforces the idea that the way we think does have a powerful influence on how we feel and, by extension, what we do. In essence, its focus is to help people change how they think, so they can change how they behave. This will reduce the number of negative behaviors they may have and give them a more ideal lifestyle in the process.

The idea behind this form of therapy is that those who struggle with emotional or behavioral problems have difficulties because of the way they view their personal experiences. In essence, it is not the experience that causes the negative behavior, but it is how their mind perceives the event. REBT focuses on changing their inner belief system to help them deal with these events better.

Another way REBT is different is that it dispels the general consensus that our past shapes who we are. The primary goal is to teach clients how to challenge deeply-entrenched beliefs they have and replace them with those that are more in line with how the way the mind really works. Like a body, the mind can adapt and recover. If successful, the result can be more than a change in the way one thinks, but also a change in how they may view their lives as a whole. They begin to have an entirely new perspective on life and how it affects them.

## What is REBT?

The theory behind this type of therapy is that humans do not act rationally in many situations. Logic is not always a part of our make-up. Computers and machines all perform their functions rationally. They take in data, analyze its logic, and provide an acceptable output. Humans, on the other hand, receive millions of tiny little inputs every day, process them very differently from machines, and instantly produce a wide variety of outputs; some of them may fit in a lot of things, but many others do not.

REBT was designed to train us to think more rationally to change our dysfunctional behaviors. Its goal is to break down our natural instincts to think irrationally, stop us from making unreasonable assumptions, and to make realistic assumptions instead. This could change our inappropriate and destructive behavior to much more positive ones. Since most of our negative thoughts and assumptions come from the irrational side of our beliefs, we react to them in inappropriate ways. It was thanks to these theories on negative thoughts that the REBT therapy was developed.

## ABCDE model of emotional disturbance

It is believed that most of our behavioral problems stem from these irrational assumptions and beliefs; thoughts that are not grounded in reality are the cause of our negative behavior. Addressing this issue, the ABCDE model of emotional disturbance was implemented.

When our goals and desires are blocked or inhibited by a particularly negative event in our lives, we hold ourselves back from accomplishing what we set out to do. This can lead to the development of these irrational beliefs. For example, an individual may apply for a job and prepares diligently for the interview. On the day of the interview, they take extra care to ensure that their appearance is perfect and they are ready to give the best impression possible. However, after all that effort, the hiring manager decides to give the job to someone else.

The logical conclusion is that, for some reason, you weren't the right fit for the job. However, someone with an irrational belief may conclude that the hiring manager knew they were just pretending, that they were a failure, or that the manager noticed their ineptitude. Some may conclude that other people had it out for them or that the "universe is against me."

Regardless of the type of negative thought you come up with, its foundation lies in the realm of unreality and can embed itself deep in the mind, triggering negative emotions and unacceptable behavior later on. To combat this type of thinking, the ABCDE model can help.

## A – The activating event

This could be any kind of event that made you develop an irrational belief. Losing a job, a car accident, an argument with your spouse. The event actually forces your mind to deal with what happened by creating an irrational thought.

## B – The irrational belief

Your mind will refer back to this belief every time a negative event comes up. When another event happens, it will trigger this negative thought process. "I'm no good, I'm a loser. I was foolish to believe I could get the job anyway."

The mind enforces this belief as a means of comfort. It is much easier to accept an irrational belief than to go through life not knowing why the distressing event actually happened in the first place.

## C – Consequences

You begin to experience the consequences of the irrational thoughts. These could be emotional, or they could be behavioral. Some consequences could be a lack of self-confidence, another could be feelings of depression, and another could be to stop trying altogether.

## D – Dispute

Eventually, you may come to recognize that your belief system is irrational, and it is the reason for your problems. You may begin to challenge those beliefs. Some people come to realize this on their own, and others may need the help of a therapist to come to this conclusion. If you have a therapist, they will give you the help you need to effectively argue with your subconscious mind and dispel these negative beliefs. They may teach you how to come up with convincing evidence that goes against your established belief system.

## E – Effect

Once you have successfully won your argument with yourself, changes will begin to appear. You may experience a boost in your self-esteem, you may be emboldened enough to apply for more jobs, or you just may find that you feel much better about yourself overall. These are the satisfying results of replacing negative thoughts with more positive ones.

Even without a therapist, the ABCDE model can be very beneficial in getting to the root of your negative thinking and behavior and give you the tools to change it.

## REBT Exercises

There are numerous exercises and techniques that can be used in this type of CBT. Some can be completed on your own, while others can only be done during group sessions or with a partner. Here are just a few of them that can give you a pretty good idea of how you can identify, challenge, and change your harmful thinking patterns:

- **How to identify and dispute irrational beliefs**
  This exercise requires the client to keep a journal cataloging their irrational thoughts. After detailing their thoughts for a period of time, they can look back and try to identify similarities and patterns that could give them a clue as to what started them down the path of irrational thinking.

  They will divide their paper into seven columns:
  - In column 1 they will write the date and the time
  - Column 2 - they will describe the situation
  - Column 3 - they write down the 'automatic' thought

- Column 4 - they write down their emotions
- Column 5 - they write down any irrational beliefs that popped up during the event
- Column 6 - they brainstorm alternative thoughts that dispute those beliefs
- Column 7 – they write the outcome

Simply by following this very simple journaling exercise, you can identify the negative thoughts and develop strong arguments designed to dispute them. When you can connect your beliefs directly to your actions and discover the triggering events and negative patterns, you arm yourself with the ability to change your behavior.

- **The consequence analysis form**
  This exercise allows you to recognize when you're experiencing consequences that resulted from your irrational beliefs. It can also help in devising a solution that targets the very core of your behavior. The REBT form is all you need.

The paper should be divided into two sections. The first section should be labeled 'Target.' In this section, you need to write down a specific problem that you're having trouble coping with. You also need to detail what your specific goals and values actually are.

In the second section, labeled 'Short-Term Consequences,' you will write down any gains you might receive based on the consequences as well as any shortcomings you might experience. These could be damage, losses, or any negative aspects that come up if you continue your unwanted behavior.

Then you will have to give each of these consequences a rating. You can use a counting system from 0 to 100 or 1 to 10, whichever works best for you.

In the third section of the paper, you will repeat the exercise you did in the second section, only this time, you will identify and rate 'Long-Term Consequences' using the same rating system.

After completing the paper, take the time to compare short-term consequences with the long-term consequences and determine if it is really beneficial for you to continue with your negative thinking and behavior, or if it is smarter to make adjustments.

- **Replacing negative beliefs**
This exercise encourages you to confront your negative automatic thoughts and belief system. It

promotes the importance of applying reason to self-critical beliefs and replacing them with more functional and realistic thoughts and habits. It is relatively simple to do. Again, all you'll need is a piece of paper.

On the top of your paper draw two boxes. In the first one you will write down 'Old belief,' and in the second box write down 'New belief.' These two boxes will become headings for the rest of the paper.

Underneath the boxes write 'Evidence to support the new belief' and under that, you will write everything that challenges your old beliefs. Try to write down at least 10 statements that support your new thoughts or may challenge the old ones. In this section, you can write down anything that supports the new positive belief system. It could be an experience you had, something you learned or observed, or something that brings into question your old belief.

Afterward, you can review what you wrote and decide if there is more evidence to support your new belief or the old one.

- **Problem formulation**
  With this exercise, you can use a rational approach
  to compare your typical response to a situation with
  a more positive response. It will help you identify
  the two different types of emotional reactions to an
  event: unhealthy vs. healthy.

  Divide the paper into three sections. In the first
  section, write down an activating event (this is
  something that triggered a negative emotional
  response).
    o Describe the event
    o Pinpoint what triggered your response
    o What sensations you had
    o Create a metaphor for the event
  In the next section, describe the negative response,
  label the emotion, and write down any thoughts or
  mental images that came with it.

  In the last section, write down the healthy response
  that could have been used in reaction to the event.
  This section could be labeled as the 'healthy'
  response and will serve as your targeted emotion.

  Afterward, compare the two scenarios and determine
  which one of them will work best for you overall.

Realize that REBT is just one form of CBT. Yet, it is an extremely effective means of training people to change their irrational thoughts. It encourages people to base their beliefs on rational thinking and use that rationality to dispel negative beliefs, replacing them with a more positive and life-fulfilling purpose that will build a person up rather than tear them down.

# Chapter 7: Dialectical Behavior Therapy (DBT)

'Dialectical Behavior Therapy,' or DBT, is another form of positive psychotherapy that is tailored more towards those people who are suffering from a borderline personality disorder.

## What is DBT?

Sometimes referred to as 'talk therapy,' DBT stresses the psychosocial components of treatment. The basic theory behind DBT is that there are people who will react to situations in a much more extreme manner than others do. These are usually the result of emotional interactions to events in their romantic, family, or social relationships.

The general idea is that there are some people whose arousal levels can increase much more quickly than that of most people. Their emotional reactions are often at a higher level, and it takes much longer for them to return to normal after an episode.

These people commonly experience extreme emotional swings, they only see the world in black-and-white, tend to find themselves in an endless line of crises, and they spend most of their life jumping from one issue to another. In most cases, they have no means of coping with these sudden emotional outbursts and, therefore, can get no relief.

There are three elements of DBT:

- **Support oriented**
  DBT can help patients identify their strong suits and utilize them so they feel better about themselves.

- **Cognitive-based**
  It helps patients identify the thoughts and beliefs that are making their lives more difficult and teaches them different ways to cope with events to make their lives become more tolerable.

- **Collaborative**
  The client and the therapist work together to root out the problems in the client's relationships through homework assignments, role-play, and self-soothing practices to use when the patients are having an emotional outburst.

Each DBT session has two primary components:

## Structured individual psychotherapy sessions

In a weekly one-on-one session with the therapist, the emphasis is on addressing problem-solving behavior and issues that may have occurred in the previous week. With these types of patients, there could be many of these problems such as issues that spring from suicidal tendencies or tendencies that lead to injuring themselves, and these will take priority. After that, they will address specific behaviors that could interrupt the therapy sessions.

The therapist focuses on teaching and reinforcing adaptive behavior with an emphasis on teaching them how to better manage their emotional trauma when it occurs rather than removing the negative experience entirely. The ultimate goal is to get the patients to improve their social skills, so they have better relationships and can interact more successfully with others.

## Group therapy sessions

In group therapy sessions, patients go through four different modules where they learn specific skills for coping with their negative patterns:

- **Mindfulness**

They are guided in observing, describing, and participating in their own behaviors. Through mindfulness exercises, they learn how to recognize what is happening in their mind, their bodies, and the emotions and how to manage those reactions better.

- **Interpersonal effectiveness**

They learn how to interact with different people in different scenarios. DBT skills in these types of sessions are very similar to those taught in many assertiveness training and problem-solving classes. They are given strategies in the proper way to ask for what they need, how to say no, and how to cope with issues of conflict.

- **Distress tolerance**

They learn how to accept distressing situations in a non-judgmental fashion, such as how to accept the reality of a situation without having to approve of it. In essence, they are learning how to survive and cope using self-soothing techniques.

- **Emotion regulation**

They learn how to identify intense emotions and cope with them better. They will have to address various aspects of emotion regulation including:

- How to properly identify and label their emotions

- How to recognize obstacles that prevent them from changing their emotions

- How to lower their vulnerability to emotions

- How to have more positive emotional experiences

- How to increase their mindfulness with their emotions

- How to react opposite of their natural tendency

- How to apply the distress tolerance strategies and techniques they have learned

While there are two primary components of DBT, the majority of the work is  done in group therapy sessions where patients can better practice the new skills and strategies they have learned. Even though it is relatively new, introduced recently in the 1980s, DBT is recognized as a gold standard form of psychological treatment for those who struggle with a borderline personality disorder.

# Chapter 8: The Evaluation Session

There is one major difference between cognitive behavioral therapy and other forms of psychotherapy. While you will have weekly sessions with your therapist, the sessions will not go on indefinitely. At some point, you will reach your final session where you will be expected to look back over the previous weeks and evaluate how you've changed.

This is an important step because, no doubt, the skills you've learned throughout your therapy have prepared you to combat your negative thoughts and helped you redirect your thinking. However, your negative habits didn't develop in a matter of weeks, and they won't be fixed in such a short period of time either. Therefore, you will have to evaluate your progress, embrace the skills that worked best for you, and carry them with you into the future because you will undoubtedly have many more battles of the mind to look forward to.

When you began your therapy, you started with specific exercises that helped you identify the specific problems that were affecting your life. Based on what was revealed in those exercises, you created a set of goals to reach for and activities that would, in time, help you achieve them. Now it's time to go back to the beginning to see how far you've come.

## Evaluate your goals

As you look back over your goals, ask yourself if you have been able to achieve them. If you haven't, how much closer are you to reaching them than you were before you began your therapy? As you reflect on your progress, mentally work your way through each therapy session and pinpoint those that you felt you learned the most from. You may need to go back through all of your homework pages, exercises, journals, and notes to remember them all and then write down what you realize after the fact.

Take special note of any changes that others may have noticed in your behavior. This can positively reinforce that it wasn't all in your head. Look for events in your life that you experienced and analyze your responses to them. Make a note of any of them that made you feel as if you were making progress, even if most of the people around you weren't aware that you were in therapy.

No doubt, analyzing your goals will reveal much about how well CBT has worked for you. Don't expect that you will have met all of your goals by the end of the therapy session, but you should be able to see some progress as you go through each one. Now, it's time to decide which of the goals you plan to continue pursuing and which ones you will adjust and make changes with.

Create a plan of action applying some of the tools and strategies you've learned to cope with your new perspective. We all need to be reminded of the progress we've made, even if we don't have negative behaviors to deal with. As you evaluate the changes you made, think of ways to carry it forward. At your last session with your therapist, you can develop a plan together that will help you address future obstacles on your own.

This should include anticipating a setback from time to time. Life is out of our control, and there will always be traumatic negative events that could send us spiraling backward if we're not careful. Determine which scenarios have the potential for triggering such an event. Now is the time to prepare for that and to develop a set of activities that will help you overcome such an obstacle.

While you won't have your therapist to guide you through life's landmines, that doesn't mean you can't have a partner or buddy to be your support. There are many advantages to including a friend or family member in your plans. It not only gives you someone to be accountable to, they can be a great source of emotional and psychological support for those times when you start to slip.

Generally, people with depressive or anxiety disorders struggle with trusting others and are more inclined to shut people out rather than invite them in. The very fact that you are considering using a partner in your continuing efforts could be a strong indication of significant progress.

And don't forget the techniques you've learned throughout the program.

As you review your lessons, you can expand your list of goals. Many who have completed CBT have realized that the lessons they applied in one area of their life can easily be applied in other areas. If you went through therapy to improve your relationships in the workplace, maybe those skills can now be extended to improve relationships in your family.

As your anxiety begins to dissipate, and depression starts to fade, you'll find that you have more time for other things. You'll be more willing to step outside your comfort zone and, in the end, you can nourish the aspects of your being that make you who you are physically, psychologically, and spiritually.

# Conclusion

It can be difficult to see the changes in your life if you're struggling to live with them. As you've gone through these pages, hopefully, you've picked up on some points that you may not have realized about yourself. CBT is one of the most modern forms of psychotherapy to date. Unlike other forms of therapy that focus on identifying the root cause of negative emotions and behaviors, it concentrates on changing an individual's thought patterns.

The general theory is that if we change the way we think or perceive the world around us, our emotions and conduct will follow. Our brain is a very complicated thing. It is sometimes described as a supercomputer, but as we have learned, it is much more than that. A computer accepts input, analyzes it, and then produces a predictable and rational output that is appropriate for the situation.

Our brains do so much more than that. If we don't understand an event or are disappointed by one, it will devise a way to help us cope with disappointment. If we experience trauma, it devises a way to help us survive it, and if life fails to meet our expectations, our brains will find a way to compensate for the loss we experienced. The problem that results from these automatic thoughts is that our brain can easily trigger negative emotions and behaviors that don't fit in with the rest of the world.

As a result, we may experience poor relationships, problems at work, poor health, and a host of other problems that we will end up struggling with. This can throw our entire life off-balance and send us spiraling out of control emotionally, psychologically, and spiritually. This is where CBT can be of immense help in teaching us how to redirect our minds and retrain them to focus on the positive things in our life, accepting reality, and the right way of handling things.

Through the pages of this book, we have learned the basics of CBT, how to get started, and how to identify those negative thoughts that often present themselves without warning. How many of us have minds that self-sabotage our efforts at every turn? But it also gave us practical strategies that will teach us how to cope better with the downside of life.

We've learned that we don't respond to the 'events' that trigger negative emotions, but we respond to how we perceive those events. Understanding this fact helps us to see how a change in our perspective in life will, by extension, change our life as a whole.

If you have gone through cognitive behavioral therapy, your therapist will probably notice your changes even before you do. They will be monitoring your progress as you go through the program. They will look at your symptoms, measure your progress in specific target areas, and assess how well you are working towards meeting your goals.

You, on the other hand, may not notice the changes as quickly. So, save all your journals, papers, notes, and homework assignments so that when you reach the end, you can look back, and you will see for yourself just how far you've come.

Every case is different. Some of you will notice a change almost immediately, while others may not see any significant progress for a while. Remember, it's all about baby steps. Taking many small steps may not seem like you're getting anywhere, but in time, they will amount to major accomplishments.

There is a reason why you picked up this book. Perhaps you or someone you care about needs a little help managing their negative feelings. If you're feeling down about yourself, lost in a world of billions, or just can't seem to turn your life around, you may very well be plagued by negative thoughts and behaviors that are getting in your way. By using the techniques taught in this book, you may find your way out of the quagmire and into a more fulfilling and promising life.

We hope that you enjoyed what we presented here and learned something from it. It is our goal to make CBT more accessible to the people who need it because we know that a majority of people don't have access to a therapist for this type of treatment. By discussing the basic fundamentals, some of the strategies and techniques used, and teaching how to apply it, we hope more and more people can change their life for the better with the help of CBT. If you are seeking a better family life, a better social life, or a better work life, we hope that this book has guided you through the basics of CBT, so you can achieve those results.

Finally, if you found this book useful in any way, a review on Amazon is always appreciated!